Read All About It!

Elizabeth Massie

Illustrated by Paul Guinan

Rigby

A Harcourt Achieve Imprint

www.Rigby.com
1-800-531-5015

Literacy by Design Leveled Readers: *Read All About It!*

ISBN-13: 978-1-4189-3913-7
ISBN-10: 1-4189-3913-7

Printed in China
1 2 3 4 5 6 7 8 985 13 12 11 10 09 08 07 06

Contents

Chapter 1
Papers for Sale!

Eleven-year-old Connor Murphy jumped back from the rattling wagon, but not in time to keep from getting splashed with dirty puddle water. His pants, shoes, and socks were soaked.

"At least my newspapers aren't muddy," he said to himself with a sigh.

Today was Connor's first day selling newspapers on the streets of San Francisco. He'd wanted to look neat and clean for the job, but now he looked careless and sloppy.

Earlier that morning, Connor had washed, dressed, and walked to Dupont Street, where Mr. Winston Chiswick brought copies of the *San Francisco Daily Press* to give out to the many newsies, the young boys who sold the papers.

Mr. Chiswick had been none too pleasant and none too patient when Connor had said, "Good morning." The man had just tossed a bundle of papers at him and said, "It will only be good when you sell all these papers, boy!"

Connor caught the papers without losing his balance, as did the other boys who had gathered around Mr. Chiswick's cart like moths to a flame.

Once the newsies had their bundles cut apart and stuffed into their shoulder bags, they hurried off to their streets. Connor waited because, as a new seller, he didn't know where he was supposed to go.

"Excuse me," Connor asked, "where should I go to sell my papers?"

Mr. Chiswick rubbed his chin as he thought and then said, "I need a boy over near Chinatown, along California Street. Do you know what to say to customers?"

"I've watched the other boys," said Connor, "and I know they shout, 'Read all about it!'"

"Yep," said Mr. Chiswick, "but you've also got to tell people today's headlines so they'll know what they're going to read all about. Try again, boy."

Connor pulled a paper from his bag, stared at the front page, and then said, "If you show me how, I'll be able to do it right."

"I don't have time for this, kid!" exclaimed Mr. Chiswick, but he grabbed a paper and read in a booming voice, "March 14, and New York City is helpless after a terrible spring blizzard! Can you do it like that?"

"Yes, sir," said Connor.

Mr. Chiswick's expression softened, for he knew Connor was an orphan and lived in an orphanage with other children who had no parents. "I guess you really need this money, being an orphan, don't you?" he said.

Connor only said, "Don't worry about me—I'll sell the papers."

Two hours later, he was at the edge of Chinatown on California Street, soaking wet, his voice hoarse from shouting "Read all about it!" and only half his papers were sold. Traffic on the street was heavy with cable cars humming along while men in top hats and women in long skirts stopped to buy Connor's papers for two cents each.

Other people passed by, but they dressed and spoke very differently from Connor's other customers. These were the citizens of Chinatown, dressed in long shirts with wide sleeves and wearing their hair in single braids. Chinatown was a strange place to Connor, somewhere he'd never been and somewhere he didn't want to go.

"A paper, please," said a voice, and Connor looked behind him to see a Chinese boy about his own age, holding out two cents.

Surprised, Connor said, "Why would you want a paper if you can't even read English?"

The Chinese boy crossed his arms, glared, and yelled, "My pennies are as good as anyone else's pennies!"

Connor shoved a paper at the boy and said, "Don't yell at me!"

The Chinese boy turned away with a sharp nod, his head held high as he walked toward one of the many alleys, or narrow streets, leading into Chinatown.

Suddenly there was a shout, and Connor turned to see a large black horse rearing up on its hind legs as the frightened man in the saddle tried to reach the dropped reins.

Chapter 2

Yee Seng
in Chinatown

The Chinese boy dropped his newspaper and raced into the street to grab the frightened horse's reins. The boy held the leather tightly until the horse quieted, and then the man grabbed back the reins and rode off without a single word of thanks.

Connor stood for a moment, impressed with the boy's bravery. Then he noticed the fallen newspaper, picked it up, and ran after the Chinese boy as he headed for the alley. Neither spoke as Connor handed the paper over, but the Chinese boy smiled.

The Chinese boy, Yee Seng, entered the alley, which was crowded with crates and barrels. Apartment buildings lined the alley, and from open windows, Yee Seng could hear babies crying and children laughing. Outside their doors, women chatted with each other as they collected rainwater from the barrels.

Clinging to building walls were banners of Chinese words advertising laundries, grocery stores, and restaurants. The scents of hot oil, soy, and fish floated on the air.

Yee Seng stepped briskly along, his newspaper under his arm, so he could get home in time to walk with his father to the factory. From noon until midnight, they sewed shirts, each of them earning a dollar a week.

He reached an old wooden building and went inside. Up three floors was the spotless two-room apartment where he lived with his father and grandparents.

Yee Seng's grandmother and grandfather, at the table cutting vegetables, nodded to Yee Seng as he came inside. Yee Seng bowed to his grandparents and greeted them, put the paper on the table, and called to his father to let him know it was time to go.

Yee Seng's father joined them in the kitchen, and father and son set off for work. The factory was nine blocks away down Wa Sheng Shong Hong—also called Washington Street—and as they walked, they talked.

"I rescued a man who was nearly thrown from his horse today," Yee Seng said, "but the man didn't thank me."

"Don't expect thanks for good deeds," said Yee Seng's father.

"He was not Chinese," said Yee Seng.

Yee Seng's father said nothing but walked on, staring straight ahead.

"A newspaper boy picked up the newspaper I dropped and brought it to me," said Yee Seng, "and he wasn't Chinese, either."

Yee Seng's father shook his head and said, "It is sad to say, but I am surprised that he helped you."

Chapter 3
Lies and Hopes

Work was long and hard at Chandler's Clothing Factory, where Yee Seng and his father operated sewing machines in a hot room filled with many other workers.

The workday seemed endless, but at last it was midnight—time to go home!

When they got home, Yee Seng and his father looked over the newspaper by lantern light. One article was about a blizzard in New York City, and one talked about a new shipping company in San Francisco.

Then Yee Seng said, "And here's another one of those terrible articles!"

"Read it," said Yee Seng's father grimly.

Yee Seng read, "Chinatown was inspected yesterday by the Board of Health, and it was determined that the place continues to be dangerous and unhealthy. Chinese people are filthy and do not care about spreading disease. The Board of Health fears that the diseases in Chinatown will spread to homes and businesses belonging to real Americans outside Chinatown."

Yee Seng's father said, "The city doesn't give us enough street cleaners, and doctors don't want to treat us, so of course there is disease!"

Yee Seng said softly, "Then we must continue to work hard, and we can hope that someday we will be respected for who we really are."

In another part of San Francisco in the Sutter Street Orphanage, Connor lay on his back in the darkness thinking about the money he'd earned that day. He had only a few nickels, but they would add up. Then he'd leave the orphanage and use the money to travel in hopes of finding his Uncle Patrick, who'd come out west in 1869 to work on the transcontinental railroad. "It would be grand," he thought, "to live in a real home with a real family, good food, and warm blankets!"

"You weren't in school today," whispered Edward from his bed next to Connor's.

"I was selling newspapers by Chinatown so I can get out of this place," said Connor.

"I wouldn't want to be near Chinatown," said Edward, "and I think those Chinese should go back to China where they belong."

"Maybe, but my family was from Ireland, so why shouldn't I go back, too?"

"It's not the same," said Edward, "and from now on, I want you to pay me a penny a day or I'll tell the teacher where you are."

Connor mumbled something and soon fell into a restless sleep.

Chapter 4
Yee Seng's Gift

Connor quickly learned that the best way to sell all of his papers was to tip his hat to the ladies and compliment the men. Sometimes Mr. Chiswick came by and said that Connor was doing a fine job. This made Connor feel good, as did the growing pile of coins under his pillow at the orphanage.

Each morning the Chinese boy bought a paper, and though Connor didn't say much to him, he wondered what the Chinese boy's life was like. Both Mr. Chiswick and Edward had said that Chinatown was dirty and crowded, that there was a lot of crime, and that the Chinese were not to be trusted.

But one day, as the Chinese boy handed Connor his pennies, he said, "My name is Choi Yee Seng, but you can call me Yee Seng."

Connor said slowly, "Mine is Connor Murphy."

Yee Seng nodded.

"Don't you go to school?" Connor asked as he dropped the coins into his pocket, pulled a paper from his bag, and handed it to Yee Seng.

Yee Seng shook his head and said, "I work with my father in a clothing factory making shirts. Don't you go to school, either?"

"No," said Connor, "because I have to work to save money so I can go find my uncle and live with him."

Yee Seng folded the paper under his arm and said, "Who do you live with now?"

Connor didn't want this boy to know that he was an orphan, so he said, "Oh, I live over on Sutter Street near Smith's Hardware Store."

A lady carrying an umbrella slowed down near Connor, looked at both boys, shook her head, and walked away.

"You have to get out of here so I can sell my papers!" Connor said to Yee Seng.

"Do you live in that orphanage on Sutter Street?" asked Yee Seng.

"I told you to leave!" said Connor.

Yee Seng spun about and left, and Connor went back to selling his papers, hot and angry, even though it was a cool March day.

"Read all about the new hotel that will be built on Stuart Street!" he called as loudly as he could through gritted teeth.

A man paid two cents and began reading one of the papers. "You'd better read more carefully," he said. "That new hotel is being built on Stockton Street, not Stuart Street."

The days that followed were cold and windy, and it was hard for Connor to stay warm in the thin jacket the people in charge of the orphanage had given him. Yee Seng bought a paper each morning and greeted Connor. One day the Chinese boy brought him a bag of cashews, but Connor didn't take them.

"I don't need your food!" he declared, but Yee Seng left the bag near the curb and went away. Before someone could step on the bag, Connor snatched it up and ate most of the nuts.

The cashews were delicious, and Connor wished he hadn't yelled at Yee Seng. He saved a few of the nuts and gave them to Edward when he got back to the orphanage that night.

The next morning, when Yee Seng came for a paper, Connor thanked him for the cashews. "I'm glad you liked them," Yee Seng said, and he pulled out of his pocket three steamed buns wrapped in paper and gave them to Connor, who ate one right away, wrapped the others tightly, and tucked them in the side of his sock.

Connor handed Yee Seng a paper, but when Yee Seng offered the money, Connor wouldn't take it. Yee Seng seemed to understand and left without another word. Connor watched as Yee Seng walked away, thinking that maybe all Chinese people weren't as bad as Edward and Mr. Chiswick said they were.

Suddenly Connor saw three big, tough-looking boys surround Yee Seng, laugh at him, and block his way so he couldn't pass.

Yee Seng's heart pounded, and his mouth went dry as the older boys yelled at him and shook their fists in his face. They were much taller than he, and they had hatred in their eyes.

"Get away from me this minute!" Yee Seng said, but the boys wouldn't leave him alone.

Then Yee Seng saw Connor running toward him and heard him shout, "Get away from him right now!"

"Look," said one of the older boys around Yee Seng, "this little paperboy likes a Chinese boy!"

Connor skidded to a stop near Yee Seng, pointed up the street past an onion cart, and said, "There are two policemen there, and they'll arrest you if you don't leave Yee Seng alone!"

The older boys laughed, but they looked doubtful, so they turned away and quickly walked off down California Street.

Yee Seng said, "Thank you for saving my life."

"I'm not sure I did that," said Connor, "but those boys had no business treating you that way."

"I want to thank you properly," said Yee Seng, "so why don't you come to my home for dinner on Sunday?"

Connor hesitated, scratched his head under his hat, and then said, "All right."

"I'll meet you at six o'clock on the corner where you sell papers," said Yee Seng.

"All right," Connor said again, though he looked very nervous.

Chapter 5
Connor in Chinatown

Yee Seng's father wasn't happy that Connor had been invited to dinner, but he said very little about it on their walks to and from the clothing factory over the next few days.

When Sunday finally arrived, Yee Seng helped his grandmother fix chicken with black bean sauce, and then they set the table with the chipped yet beautiful dishes that Yee Seng's grandparents had brought 15 years earlier from China.

Connor, with his hat on his head and his bag over his shoulder, was waiting for Yee Seng at six o'clock.

"Are you hungry?" asked Yee Seng, and then he realized that it wasn't a polite question, so he said, "My grandmother makes wonderful meals, and I get hungry just thinking about them!"

On the way through Chinatown, Yee Seng had to walk slowly because Connor wanted to look at everything they passed. On one street there was a festival, and Connor was startled but pleased by the fireworks and lanterns.

At Yee Seng's apartment, Connor was greeted by Yee Seng's father and grandparents. Connor pulled the last paper from his pack and presented it to Yee Seng's father.

"A small gift for inviting me," said Connor, and Yee Seng's father politely accepted it without smiling.

During dinner Connor showed Yee Seng's family the crumpled old photo of his uncle that he carried in his pocket. Connor explained that the picture had been taken just before Uncle Patrick left to work on the railroad, and that Connor and his parents had not come to California until 1880. Connor sadly continued by adding that his parents had died in an apartment fire a few months after they got to San Francisco, and then Connor was placed in an orphanage before Uncle Patrick could be found. Now Connor was determined to find his father's oldest brother.

"There are workers at our factory who worked on the railroad," said Yee Seng's father, "and I will ask if they know of your uncle."

"That would be good," said Connor with a big grin, and this time Yee Seng's father smiled back.

After dinner, Yee Seng took the paper Connor had brought and read an article, pausing at times to translate for his grandparents, about a fire on Fisherman's Wharf. Everyone listened to the story of a careless restaurant cook who let sparks from his kitchen get out of control and burn down his building and the warehouse next to it.

Connor said to Yee Seng, "How did you learn to read English if you don't go to school?"

"I taught myself," said Yee Seng, "and my father did the same because we believe that it is important to be able to know what is going on in our city and our country. When did you learn to read, Connor?"

Connor looked suddenly uncomfortable and said, "I have to get back to the orphanage before they do bed count, or I'll be in big trouble!"

Yee Seng walked Connor out of Chinatown, asking him several times along the way about his school, but Connor kept ignoring Yee Seng's questions. Then Yee Seng thought, "I'll bet Connor Murphy can't read at all!"

Chapter 6
Connor's Secret

It had started to rain by the time Connor was alone on California Street, so he pulled his jacket tighter around him and headed across the road, avoiding a horse and rider as raindrops trickled down his nose to his chin.

"Hey there, boy!" called a man, and Connor looked up to see Mr. Chiswick in his cart, looking furious.

"Don't worry," said Connor. "I sold all my papers today."

"That's not what bothers me," said Mr. Chiswick. "It's seeing you with a Chinese boy. Don't you know how dangerous and dirty those people are?"

"Yee Seng and his family aren't dirty or dangerous," said Connor.

Mr. Chiswick shook his finger at Connor and said, "It doesn't look good for one of our boys to be friendly to those people, so you'd better be staying away from them if you want to keep your job."

Connor started to protest, but Mr. Chiswick just drove off in the rain.

Back at the orphanage, Connor climbed onto the roof of a shed and into the bedroom window. The other boys were getting ready for bed, and only Edward and Timothy noticed him sneak in.

"You missed dinner," said Edward, "but everyone thinks you were sick in bed."

"You'd better look sick for bed count," said Timothy, "or you'll have some explaining to do!"

When a teacher came in, Connor pretended to groan softly in his sleep, and the teacher left shaking his head.

Connor kept an eye out for Mr. Chiswick over the next few days, wanting to talk to Yee Seng, but not wanting his boss to find out.

One morning Yee Seng appeared on California Street with a smile and a slip of paper. He handed it to Connor and said, "What do you think about this?"

Connor shrugged and replied, "I have to watch for customers, so just read it to me."

Yee Seng paused and then said, "You can't read it, can you?"

Connor opened and closed his mouth a few times and finally admitted, "I never could learn to read when I was in school, so I guess I can't learn at all."

Yee Seng shook his head and said, "You can learn because you've learned other things, and reading might help you find your uncle."

"How would reading help me find Uncle Patrick?" asked Connor.

Yee Seng said, "At work yesterday, my father asked if anyone knew Patrick Murphy who had worked on the railroad, and one worker wrote down the address of a man named Joseph Wheeler. He thinks Mr. Wheeler and your uncle were friends. If you could read the address on this note, you could find Joseph Wheeler, and he might know where your uncle is."

"But since you can read, you'll help me find him, won't you?"

Yee Seng nodded and said, "I will meet you tomorrow morning at six on the corner of Bush and Rose Streets."

That night Connor lay awake thinking that if Joseph Wheeler knew where to find Uncle Patrick, Connor's troubles would be over. He also thought about what Yee Seng had said about reading being helpful, but could Connor really learn?

At six the next morning, Yee Seng was standing on the corner as Connor walked up. The sun was barely up, and dogs barked from behind a heavy iron fence.

Connor knocked on the door with the number 356, and a man of about 50 slowly opened the door and squinted at him.

Chapter 7
Truths to Learn

"Mr. Wheeler, sir," said Connor to the man at the door, "my name is Connor Murphy. Do you remember a man named Patrick Murphy who worked on the transcontinental railroad?"

The man rubbed his eyes and said, "Well, last time I heard about good old Patrick Murphy he was working at the docks on Central Wharf on some fishing boat. Why?"

But Connor was already running for the street and shouting to Yee Seng, "Hurry to the bay!"

The San Francisco Bay harbor was a busy place with warehouses, docks, and ships of all shapes and sizes. Seagulls flew in circles, searching for scraps, and fishermen called to each other from their decks.

Connor and Yee Seng walked along Central Wharf, asking if anyone knew Patrick Murphy, but most of the workers ignored them or said they didn't know the man.

"We've had no luck at all, and I have to pick up my papers in half an hour!" said Connor.

"You have to be patient," said Yee Seng, "because most good things take time."

Unhappy and a little angry, Connor kicked an old bottle out of the way and headed away from the wharf with Yee Seng beside him.

"Hey, were you asking about Patrick Murphy?" shouted someone from behind, and Connor turned to see a young man in an apron and a fisherman's hat waving his hands.

Connor stopped in his tracks as the young man trotted up to him, wiping his fishy hands on his apron. "His son, Liam, worked with me on the fishing boat *Sally Green.*"

"Patrick Murphy is my father's brother," Connor said, "and he left home when he was 17 to work on the railroad. You say his son used to work with you—where is he now?"

"Liam still works on a fishing boat here in the bay, but I'm not sure which one. Patrick left San Francisco after his wife died, but he might be back now—just needed some time to think, I guess."

"He left," Connor said, feeling suddenly a bit dazed. Connor lowered himself down on an old fish crate.

"But like I said, he might be back," encouraged the young man.

Connor went back to selling papers that day, wondering whether he would find his uncle and what his cousin was like.

"I *will* learn to read," he told himself as he headed back to the orphanage that afternoon. "That way I'll know what is going on around me, and I'll have a better chance of finding my cousin!"

Chapter 8
Connor's Choice

Yee Seng gave Connor reading lessons as often as he could, and Connor was becoming more comfortable with the sights, sounds, and people of Chinatown. He sat at Yee Seng's table while Yee Seng patiently taught him simple words, and it surprised Connor to find out that wanting to learn made him better able to learn.

When the lessons were done, Connor would go down by the bay and ask about Liam Murphy, but no one he talked to knew Liam.

"I want to learn to write, too," said Connor to Yee Seng one night in June, "so I can put a notice in the newspaper asking for information about my cousin."

Yee Seng's father, who was sipping tea at the table, smiled and said, "That's a fine idea, Connor."

Each day Connor practiced reading newspaper articles as he stood on the corner selling his papers, and each day it got a little easier to understand the words.

The more Connor read, the more he noticed things he didn't like. In almost every issue of the *San Francisco Daily Press,* there was an article that said something hateful about the

Chinese people, such as calling them lazy, uneducated, or dirty. Connor read these with growing disgust. Why did so many people hate the Chinese, and why was he selling papers that spread lies about his friends?

"Well," said Mr. Chiswick as he tossed Connor's daily bundle of newspapers at him on the street, "you must have been learning your job pretty well because you never have a paper left over!"

Connor cut the string, picked up a paper, and flipped through until he found what he was looking for.

"Read all about it," he read aloud. "Chinese Responsible for More Violence in San Francisco."

Mr. Chiswick tucked his shirt into his trousers, shrugged, and said, "Why are you reading that to me, boy?"

"Why is this paper saying terrible things about the Chinese people," Connor asked, "when they aren't any worse nor any better than anyone else?"

"Newspapers want to sell a lot of papers and make lots of money," said Mr. Chiswick. "Most people want to read what they believe, and they believe the Chinese are dangerous, so that's what newspapers tell them. Those articles help sell papers and help you earn your money!"

"Not any more!" said Connor, and he knew as he threw the bundle of papers on the ground that his life was going to change.

That night Connor was waiting in front of Yee Seng's apartment when Yee Seng and his father got home from work. The two invited Connor inside and gave him tea before they asked him why he looked so sad.

Finally Connor said, "I didn't know that the newspapers said such bad things about you and the others of Chinatown. Why do you even buy these newspapers?"

"We need to know what others think," said Yee Seng's father, "so we can be prepared for what might happen to us here."

Connor put his head in his hands and said, "I'm so sorry I sold those papers! And now I have quit my job, so I'll have no way to make money to leave the orphanage."

"You can live here until you find your cousin if you'd like," said Yee Seng's father.

"And I'll help you find him," said Yee Seng.

For many moments, Connor was silent. Then he smiled and said, "We will find Liam and we'll find Uncle Patrick, too. Until that day comes, I'll have a family right here!"